DAVID'S HOPE

PAMELA YOSS COOPER

David's Hope
by Pamela Yoss Cooper

Printed in the United States of America.

Edited by Xulon Press.

ISBN 9781498499750

www.xulonpress.com

Dedication

This book is in honor of my Lord Jesus Christ.
I dedicate this book to my sons, Brian Morgan
and Chris Cooper, and to family and friends.

Special thanks to Jennifer Oliver and
Gail Strother for their editing support.

Contents

Introduction

I am honored to be able to share God's wonder through my husband David's struggle for a second chance in life. David and our family had to suffer through some difficult trials, but knowing God was with us and caring for our needs made the dark days brighter. I believe God is still using David's liver transplant testimony to minister to lost souls. David's survival is a true testament of God's healing powers and everlasting love.

The emotional roller coaster began the night we received a call from MCV Hospital, informing us that a liver was available. We waited for six long months for this call. The few hours David and I spent together prepping for surgery was precious and priceless. The conversation between us was short, but intense. We reminisced about how God brought the two of us together and the love that we shared for each other and the Lord. We were both frightened, but never felt alone. I remember staring out of the hospital window looking at the interstate and feeling like I was in another world. Several times during the night, David requested I call our church and ask for prayer. I prayed every day for a healing miracle from God. As David's condition turned for the worse, I thought maybe God did not hear my prayer, but I still waited for His answer. I finally realized the answer to my prayer was a miracle from God that was witnessed by hundreds of people. So many people accepted the Lord, and their lives were changed forever through David's suffering and miracles.

I pray this little book of hope will dwell in your heart and that your life will be touched with the love of our Heavenly Father.

"Be joyful always; pray continually; give thanks in all circumstances, for this is God's will for you in Christ Jesus."– 1 Thessalonians 5:16-18

1

Summer of 1991

A t age thirty-eight, David was physically fit and ran five miles a day. He was active in the community as a football and baseball assistant coach and worked full-time as a building inspector for Chesterfield County, Virginia. David was a wonderful and loving husband and a fabulous father to our sons, Brian and Chris.

He started to notice his vision was worse and that he coughed up blood more regularly. I knew something was seriously wrong due to the yellowing of his eyes and skin. I kept encouraging him to go to the doctor, but he refused.

David stopped running because of his weakness, but still, he continued to work. One night, I followed as he dashed to the bathroom. I stood in awe while watching him vomit thick red blood into the toilet. Where was the blood coming from, and would it ever stop? I remember screaming in panic and demanding he let me take him to the emergency room, and finally, he agreed.

The trip to Chippenham Hospital was a blur. I remember putting the two boys in the car and grabbing towels for David to use to try to stop the bleeding. At this point, blood streamed from his nose and mouth. I had to be strong for the boys, but inside, I was scared and my nerves were shot. My stomach quivered.

Upon arrival at the emergency room, he was seen by several Southern Health Insurance-approved physicians. He was diagnosed with liver disease and was referred to the Medical College of Virginia (MCV) in Richmond, Virginia, for consultation with a liver specialist. At that time, David had health insurance with Southern Health and secondary coverage with my health insurance, Metropolitan Insurance Company, under Reynolds Metals Company's plan.

The result from MCV was that David had Hepatitis C and needed a liver transplant. I immediately called Southern Health Insurance for approval for this costly operation. I was informed David had to travel to Wisconsin to receive his liver, and Southern Health would only cover the cost if we followed their procedures.

After sending David for numerous medical opinions, which were given by Southern Health-approved physicians, the doctors all agreed David's serious health condition would not allow him to travel to Wisconsin, and MCV hospital was recommended. I immediately called Metropolitan Insurance to ask for guidance in this life-or-death situation. On December 20, 1991, Metropolitan made the decision to cover David's procedure at MCV.

This is where the nine-year insurance battle started. All I wanted to do was save my husband's life. His health condition was fragile, and the doctors explained to me that he would not survive the cabin pressure during the flight to Wisconsin. Also, I needed to keep my job in Richmond with Reynolds Metals Company to support my family and to uphold my benefits. The next issue was that I had two children—Brian, age fourteen, and Chris, age six—who were in school. Who would take care of them while I was in Wisconsin? My mind was racing trying to figure out all the details. I was so overwhelmed and torn in so many directions. I needed a miracle and prayed daily that God would hear my prayers.

The next step was to wait for the perfect liver to save his life. As soon as David's employer heard about the news of his illness and the needed transplant, his coworkers went to work, promoting organ donation and blood drives in David's honor.

On March 9, 1992, a blood drive was held in David's honor at Reynolds Metals Packaging Technical Center on Reymet Road in Chesterfield, Virginia. I wasn't sure if anyone would take the time out of a busy production schedule to give blood. I was shocked sixty-five donors registered, which provided sixty donations. The majority of blood donations were separated into three different components for transfusions (red cells, plasma, and platelets), so it is possible the drive helped up to 180 different patients.

Having my coworkers show so much compassion, for not only David, but others, filled my heart with joy. I remember going back to my office with tears of joy flowing down my face. I finally felt I could do something amid the turmoil to make a difference in someone else's life. Just maybe some of these donations would be available for David's liver transplant.

I thanked God for the opportunity to promote this blood drive at work and praised Him for the acts of kindness displayed by my coworkers. I will never forget the many hugs and statements of encouragement I received.

I finally realized anything is possible with God. Put Him first, and He will bless you. I am so grateful for His unconditional love, mercy, and grace.

"Jesus replied, 'What is impossible with men is possible with God.'"–Luke 18:27

2

The Journey Begins

June 29, 1992, the night before Father's Day, felt extremely dark and cold even though it was summer. David had a liver transplant the next day, which was not successful. He was expected to be the ideal patient because he was young, strong, and fairly healthy for a Hepatitis C patient. David had renal failure. All the surgeons were surprised when his body rejected the organ and he had an allergic reaction to the antirejection medicines.

In the family waiting room, a strange woman dressed in green surgical clothes rushed into the room asking for a Mrs. Cooper. When my face met hers, she said, "I'm sorry."

I stood in the middle of the floor frozen, my face blank, and my mind racing. In a panic, I shouted, "What did you say?"

Without emotion, she briefly explained to me that David had died and was brought back to life. The nurse explained that Dr. Fisher, David's surgeon, only had twenty-four hours to find another liver for David to have a chance to survive.

I remember running down the hospital hall trembling and crying, but I could not hear anything. I felt like I was moving in slow motion. At that moment, David's parents, Bonnie and Al, came down the hall and asked how David was doing.

I shouted, "He died!"

David's parents were coming in from a fishing trip and were not up-to-date about the surgery or his condition. I should have been more sensitive regarding my response, but I was frantic and devastated.

I immediately went into shock and wept. I was brought back to reality when a nurse grabbed and held me in her arms as we both wept. I looked up and recognized Angela. She came to my rescue. I just needed someone to hug me and say everything would be all right. Angela had a bubbly personality and connected with David when they met at pre-op. She and David were born in New York, and they constantly teased each other about being a Yankee. She catered to David's needs, which made me secure about his hospital care. Due to Angela's compassion and kindness, we called her "our New York angel."

Angela pulled my mother and me into a small room beside the nurses' station. There were a few chairs and a blackboard with a list of patient names and their statuses. All I could focus on was "Cooper." Under David's name was a list of medical terms and numbers I did not understand. I remember staring at the board, praying that someone would explain his status. I had this extreme urge to see David, hold him, and tell him everything was going to be all right. While I was in a world of panic and confusion, my mother took control. She called her minister, Tom Sweat, from Ramsey United Methodist Church. Tom was close to our family, and my mother knew I needed his support and prayers.

Before I knew it, Tom slid into the tiny room dressed in shorts, a T-shirt, and loafers. He was at a Father's Day picnic with his family and left hurriedly to come to my rescue. Tom's face was pale due to his concern, but under the circumstances, he managed to smile just for me. I always told him his smile brightened the day. Tom held me while I cried, and he whispered encouraging Scripture in my ear. His voice and words calmed my soul so I could think clearly and face reality. I had to be strong for David and our sons.

Shortly after Tom left, Dr. Lee entered the room. Dr. Lee was a renowned transplant surgeon who happened to be at MCV to assist, if needed, with David's surgery. He stood in front of the blackboard studying the data and said nothing. After a few moments, he turned with his head tucked and left the room. At that moment, I felt there was no hope for David's survival. My mother continued to be by my side, constantly holding my hand and reminding me of our loving God, His miracles, and His love for us. I desperately waited to see Dr. Robert Fisher, but no doctor came.

June 20, 1992 ended. The nurses instructed me to go home and rest. They repeatedly advised me to check the battery of my beeper and to stay close to home so the hospital could reach me. I had worn a beeper for six months and panicked every time it beeped. It took six months for David to receive the first liver, so how in the world could another organ be available within twenty-four hours? I was scared and felt hopeless.

I cried so hard on the way home from the hospital that I could not see the road. I feared facing our youngest son, Chris. As I walked up the steps of my home, I went over in my mind the answers to the questions he might ask. I had to fight back the tears and put on a happy face for him.

Brian, my eldest son, was away on a tobacco farm with his best friend Johnny Clements. Debbie, Johnny's mother, reassured me that Brian would be better off emotionally to spend some time with Johnny working on his grandfather's tobacco farm in Charlotte County, Virginia. Debbie took care of Brian like he was her second son. She made sure that I knew Brian was in a safe place and was welcomed with open arms. Johnny and Brian bonded even more through the hard sunup-to-sundown labor on the farm.

During his stay, Brian called me for a nightly update of David's condition. I kept reinforcing how much I loved him and that God would take care of all of us until David came home. I knew Brian was going through a rough time, especially going through puberty and dealing with his stepfather's illness. Brian loved David, and many times he told me they were best friends.

Even the night David was called to report to the hospital for the transplant, he gave Brian a precious gift. David wore a gold cross necklace, which was a wedding gift from me. He had never removed it from his neck. That night, David removed the necklace, placed it around Brian's neck, and told him how much he loved him. Brian's eyes filled with tears as they hugged. David told Brian to take care of Chris and me.

My mother had bathed Chris and waited for my return. When I opened the door, Chris immediately jumped in my arms and asked about David. I told him he asleep and hopefully, in a few days, he could see him.

I tucked Chris into bed and we said our prayers. The whole prayer, Chris continually asked God to make his daddy better. I prayed silently that Chris would not feel my tears on his face as I leaned over to kiss him good night.

When I returned to the kitchen, my mother was at the kitchen table crying. She said, "Pam, it hurts me to see you go through this pain." She probably was reminiscing about the days my father struggled with cancer and the pain our family felt. We hugged and wept uncontrollably until the beeper I wore on my hip interrupted us. I remember looking at the clock, and it read 11:00 p.m.

The awaited phone call was received, and the response was unbelievable. The person on the other end said, "Mrs. Cooper, we found David a liver, and it is perfect." I was informed Dr. Fisher was on his way to Chicago to receive the organ and instructed MCV to call me and to prepare for David's surgery. I was told by MCV that Dr. Fisher had frantically called around the world looking for a liver for David. He called a Catholic hospital in Chicago where he once practiced and found a female patient on life support with no brain activity for months.

Dr. Fisher flew to Chicago to speak to the parents of this patient as well as hospital officials to see if they would be willing to end life support and donate her organs. With wrenching hearts, the parents agreed to let their daughter go. The staff at the hospital had to decide who would receive the patient's liver. There were five candidates for this liver, and only one was chosen. And that was David Cooper from Richmond, Virginia.

I asked Dr. Fisher, "Why David?"

He said, "God had put David's name on it."

It was a perfect match with exception to size, and David had a better chance of surviving the surgery than the other candidates.

How thankful and blessed I felt at that moment but at the same time, saddened for the donor's family. I had mixed emotions. I was sad someone had to die, but happy David had a second chance at life.

After the phone call, I realized I wanted to rally for organ donations. I tucked that thought in the back of my mind for plans in the future. I began visualizing Dr. Fisher procuring the liver in flight and placing it in a cooler for delivery. I was excited, but scared. I knew David's body was weak, and I hoped his body continued to function until the new organ arrived.

Waiting for the second transplant felt like an eternity. I prayed constantly for God's protection, guidance, and strength. Everything was in God's hands, so I had to be patient and continue to trust Him.

"Ask and it will be given to you; seek and you will find; knock and the door will be opened to you."
– Matthew 7:7

3

The Second Transplant

After the second transplant, the doctors informed me that David probably would not live through the night. I immediately called my church, the West End Assembly of God (WEAG). I knew in my heart that prayer was the answer, and David needed those prayers immediately.

I left a message early in the morning on the church's answering machine that David needed prayer. At the following Sunday service, the whole congregation joined hands and prayed for David's healing and for his life. To my surprise, that same Sunday afternoon, the waiting room of the trauma unit at MCV hospital overflowed with our church family. The hospital staff must have thought this was David's last day of life, so they let hundreds of people come into his room to pay their last respects. How odd, because the day before, only family members were allowed with sanitary masks and dress. I guess the physicians entitled this day as David's last farewell.

I watched for hours as people paraded around his comatose body. His body was so swollen; it looked like he weighed three hundred pounds. He panted with each breath to survive. I think God told him to fight for his life because He had plans for him.

Groups of people surrounded him, and they joined hands in prayer, praise, and worship. You could hear a pin drop in this usually noisy and busy trauma unit. God was there. The nursing staff and physicians dropped to their knees in prayer. The next day, I heard them say they never believed, but now they do. It was the first time some of them had ever prayed. Yes, God moved in that whole hospital that day.

Our pastors approached me to ask if David had been saved. I smiled and responded, with tears running down my face, that David was with God, whether in heaven or on earth. David loved the Lord, and his relationship with Him had only begun.

Later that evening, as the crowd cleared, Dr. Fisher called our family into the conference room. We all stared at his face with hope of good news. Dr. Fisher announced the fight was over. He instructed us to make funeral plans immediately because he would not live through the night.

The look on our family members' faces was inexplicable. David's mother looked at me and said, "This is not good." I remember the room becoming extremely quiet as I reached for a nearby trashcan to vomit. I guess, at that time, my body reacted to the stress, exhaustion, and sadness that were buried in my heart. I tried so hard to be positive, upbeat, and strong for others, especially our two sons.

That night, I don't even remember driving home on I-95. When I reached the house, I sat in the driveway for approximately thirty minutes because I was so weak, I could not even open the car door. Upon entering the house, I made sure the boys were tucked in their beds, and I listened to the most precious prayers I have ever heard. Brian prayed that his father would live to grow old with him. Chris prayed for David to get well so they could play football together. God had His ears on!

I got into the shower and cried for what felt like hours. I definitely did not want the boys to hear me cry. I needed to remain strong for them. As I got into bed, the doorbell rang. There stood my precious sister, Sandy.

She grabbed me and hugged me, and we both wept. Sandy has always been my guardian angel, and I know God sent her to me that night. She decided to get in the bed with me and talk me to sleep. It worked. I fell into a deep sleep for the first time in a great while. Sandy knew I had to sleep because the whole family had been instructed to go to MCV the next morning to make arrangements for the removal of David's body.

Sandy witnessed me jumping up in the bed and facing the door of the bedroom. I said nothing, and my face glowed. She thought I was hyperventilating, so she tried to help me. She told me later that my body was stiff, but I had a peaceful look on my face.

I heard David calling my name. When I looked at the doorway, I witnessed the brightest light I have ever seen. I was drawn into this light and not afraid. Someone spoke to me in another language. The voice was strong, but kind and loving. The message was translated for me.

The message was, "Trust and believe in me, and everything will be all right."

After the conversation was over, Sandy said I calmly lay down in the bed and went into a peaceful sleep. Today, I know that message came from the Holy Spirit. That's right: God sent His Spirit to give me this message.

The next morning, my whole family was in front of my house. My brother Chris and his wife, Gail, were anxious to hold me. As we packed into several cars, I was happy and singing. My family thought I had gone crazy through the night and wondered if they needed to call the doctor for medication.

Everyone was so depressed and sad. My neighbors witnessed this and had determined David had already passed away. I sat in the back of a big Cadillac and kept saying, "Trust and believe in me, and everything will be all right."

When we got to the hospital, Dr. Fisher ran out of the trauma unit, yelling, "It is a miracle from God. David is alive!"

He grabbed me and twirled me around and around. Dr. Fisher stated no human could live through the multiple surgeries and infections. David was so alive that Dr. Fisher went on vacation. I was shocked, but happy for him because he had worked many hours trying to keep David alive. Dr. Fisher stated in the hospital hallway that David was in God's hands.

While Dr. Fisher was on vacation, David took a turn for the worse. He got an infection in the lungs. The staff again prepared me for his death. Dr. Fisher was called and informed of David's status. He and other hospital specialists discussed his condition and decided David would not be alive when Dr. Fisher returned to the hospital from vacation.

God had other plans. David pulled out of distress and was finally moved to a regular room after months and months in the trauma unit. We finally had hope!

"Many, O Lord my God, are wonders you have done. The things you planned for us no one can recount to you; were I to speak and tell of them, they would be too many to declare." –Psalm 40:5

4

Friends to the Rescue

———————— ⌒꙰⌒ ————————

M any times during this ordeal, I felt lost and nobody
knew how my heart was breaking. It was proven
time after time that I was neither lost nor alone. David's
friends and our families were always a phone call away. I
received numerous calls from David's high school friends
who heard about his illness through a newspaper article.
Manchester class of '71 volunteered to have fundraisers,
blood drives, and whatever was necessary to help David.
Many classmates visited David in the hospital trauma
unit on a weekly basis, even though he was in a medically
induced coma. They prayed over him and talked as if he
was awake to encourage him to fight for his life.

A special classmate, Valerie Howard, was constantly
on the scene to help our family. Valerie reconciled her
friendship with David through her husband, Eddie. Eddie
and David coached T-ball and football together for Salem
Church Athletic Association. Eddie's son Travis and our
son Chris became best friends. Every weekend we were

busy on the ball field, but new friendships were developed among caring parents. Another couple, Tammy and Rocky Alexander, were among the group who became good friends of ours.

When I shared the news of David's illness with the athletic association parents, Valerie and Tammy came to the rescue. These ladies made a surprise visit to my house one morning with big grins on their faces. Laughing and grinning were not unusual because both were always mischievous and up to something to make me laugh. They grabbed me, gave me a big group hug, and instructed they were going to help. They repeatedly said to me, "Let's do something to help you, David, Chris, and Brian." In the middle of our front yard, they anxiously rattled ideas and plans for helping our family. They insisted David's story must be made public to increase awareness for organ donation. Both these ladies agreed that fundraising events were necessary to prepare for David's homecoming accommodations and to assist with his medical needs.

Valerie and Tammy went to work. They worked tirelessly for months preparing for the first event, which was a Putt-Putt marathon, scheduled for July 23, 1992, from 9:00 p.m. until 1:00 a.m. This fundraiser was sponsored by Salem Church Athletic Association, and all proceeds went to the David Cooper Fund.

I was shocked at the amount of support received that night at Midlothian Putt-Putt. Hundreds of people arrived to play Putt-Putt in David's honor. Complete strangers rallied on David's behalf, wearing organ donation pins and comforting me with words of encouragement. The crowd of people showed continuous enthusiasm through the night. Not once during the event did Valerie and Tammy look tired or weary. They constantly smiled, laughed, and encouraged people to support the cause. Before the event ended, I knew in my heart that my family would make it with the loving support of people like Valerie and Tammy.

On that same weekend, Tammy and Valerie scheduled a softball-baseball tournament from 9:00 a.m. to 7:00 p.m. at Lloyd C. Bird High School. It promised action on four fields, with adult men's and coed teams playing softball and youth teams playing baseball. Youth teams would play a double-elimination tournament (each team played until it lost twice). Adult teams were guaranteed four games. For spectators, there were plenty of concessions and prize drawings throughout the day for merchandise donated by local businesses.

Proceeds from both events would go to the David Cooper Transplant Fund. I will always remember the event participants playing their hearts out at each game and wearing Cooper T-shirts. At the award presentation, there was not one dry eye in that pavilion. Many of the players hugged me and wished me well as they raised the trophies and chanted, "Cooper, Cooper, Cooper."

After the event, everyone went to Valerie's house for refreshments and a nice, cool dip in their pool. Near the end of the night, Valerie and Tammy presented me with a huge paper check reflecting a two-thousand-dollar donation. I will never forget the hard work and dedication of Valerie and Tammy. Being around these upbeat ladies and having fun planning the event was a diversion from all the sadness and heartache of David's illness.

Words cannot express my gratitude for these two ladies. They will always be my true friends. Their actions inspired me to pay it forward or pass the love.

"As iron sharpens iron, so one person sharpens another." – Proverbs 27:17

5

Intensive Care Nightmares

———— ⌑ ————

David was immediately placed in MCV's intensive care unit after the second transplant. The area was loud, confusing, and scary at the same time. The pod had individual patient rooms connected to the main nurses' station. Each patient had an information board outside their room window that faced the nurses' station.

David was a sight to behold. I was so grateful to God that he lived through the lengthy surgery. He was connected to tubes, machines, and monitors, with alarms going off constantly. His body struggled with every breath. His chest was open for drainage, and all I could do was stare at the Mercedes-shaped incision. I was hurt to see him suffering in a coma. I wanted him to open his eyes and look into mine so I could tell him that I loved him with all my heart. I also wanted him to see his boys, Chris and Brian. I wanted him to know we were his cheerleaders, and that we were behind him 100 percent.

I pondered how long it would take before he spoke to me. I was told if he lived through this recovery period, he might be in a vegetative state with little quality of life. I constantly checked his blood pressure and his respiratory charts. I made sure I constantly touched him, in hopes that he knew I was there.

The numbers on his chart were foreign to me. I paid attention to the conversations at the nurses' station and the quick spurts of information from the doctors as they passed David's room.

The nursing staff kept me abreast of his bowel functions and alerted me of concerns. David's kidneys were failing, and the doctor said he might need a kidney transplant. I fell into panic mode and wondered how he would survive another transplant. I prayed immediately for God to touch and heal his kidneys. I prayed every day for his body to function properly. I just wanted him to have a bowel movement, to urinate, or to show some signs that his body could work on its own.

I could not wait to hear David's voice. I waited for months, hoping he would wake up and smile at me. I never wanted to leave him, because I thought I would miss a movement of his hands or legs, or even that he'd make a slight effort to smile.

After months in an induced coma, the doctors determined David would not live long; there had been little improvement. They had the nerve to tell me to pull the plug! I was not going to give up and pull his respiratory cord. I told the staff that David's life was in God's hands, and that He decides when it's time for someone to go home.

Every time I went to his bedside, I felt there was no hope from the doctor's staff. One day, I was in his room with my mother when he had a tiny bowel movement in our presence. I was so excited that I screamed, "He pooped!" Mother and I fought each other to be the first to wipe his buttocks. We were both so excited. At that moment, I had renewed hope that he would be all right.

The days that were spent in the intensive care unit turned into long months. It appeared David would never leave the unit or the hospital. One Sunday afternoon, I decided to leave him and return home for some rest. Upon arriving at home, I received a call from my sister to come to her house for dinner. It had been a long time since I spent quality time with my family outside of the hospital. I agreed and looked forward to seeing family members for some good food, hugs, and hopefully, some laughs.

As soon as I arrived at my sister's home, my beeper sounded. That sound usually made my heart sink, thinking of only the worst for David. To my surprise, I called the hospital and then leaped for joy. I screamed, "David is awake!" as I flew out the door and ran to my car. I could not get to the hospital fast enough. It appeared God had made all the stoplights turn green to quicken my journey from Chesterfield County to Broad Street in Richmond.

I ran into David's room with hopes of hearing him say, "Pam, I love you. Come here and give me a kiss." Upon reaching his bedside, I stopped dead in my tracks when I saw his face. He did not smile nor speak and looked at me as if I was a stranger. My heart was broken, and my knees were weak. I felt like my body WOULD crumble into tiny pieces onto the floor by my heart pounding in my chest. I could not believe what I was experiencing.

Where was my husband? What happened to the love of my life, my soul mate?

The nurses explained to me that David needed to learn how to walk, talk, and eat again. He had no muscle strength, and therapy would be long and hard. David was still on morphine, had a tracheotomy, and could only communicate with a small chalkboard, which was beside him in the bed. He was so weak and shaky that I could not make out his handwriting on the board.

As I continued to stare at him with disbelief, he looked mean and wrote on the board that I had to leave because I was a Nazi and not allowed in his room anymore. He wrote that he hated me. Later on after full recovery, David explained to me that morphine made him think and do crazy things. He believed there was a war going on between Germany and Russia and that I was the enemy.

There was a large windowsill in David's room that housed flowers and cards. Our son, Chris, liked to sit in the windowsill to look at David and also the traffic below on I-95. One evening, when Chris was in the window area, David's face turned red, and his eyes bulged as he franticly grabbed the chalk and wrote on the board to remove Chris immediately before he fell to his death. David obviously could not rationalize Chris was in the hospital beside him and was safe.

That same evening, David wrote on the board, "No more morphine," as tears rolled down his face. We had celebrated his birthday with hospital staff days before with cake, balloons, and laughter. I guess the morphine prevented him from understanding what we were doing, but one thing was sure: he hated the shiny silver balloons in his room. He wrote to put the scary dancing men in his closet. I responded to his request, pulled the balloons from the ceiling, and placed them in the closet. Maybe now he would feel safe and fall asleep in peace.

Immediately, I rushed to the nurses' station to request David receive no more morphine. David's chart was noted following the doctor's review and approval. After stopping the morphine, I started to see David come to life. We still had a long way to go, but we were now a team fighting for life.

Months after David's recovery, I begged him to explain to me his journey through the coma stage. Our pastor, John Hershman, could not wait to speak to David about his death experience. John wanted to know all the wonderful details of heaven. I remember David looking at Pastor Hershman with concern and fear because he didn't experience heaven.

David responded to John by saying, "As I lay in an unconscious state with my body saturated with morphine, I had vivid dreams in living color." David excitedly told Pastor Hershman the stories. Typically, David's dreams were of no significance, but he believed these dreams were because they were spiritually based. In the past, David's dreams were always unfinished and not etched in his memory bank, but he remembers all of these from start to finish in great detail.

The first dream started in a cave, and David floated down the Amazon River, which was more like a creek. He searched for a new beginning, a fresh start from the darkened past. David explained to his passenger in the canoe—Michael Jackson—that he wanted the past to be behind him and to forget the wasted portion of his past life. David felt there was a destination within sight. While still rowing, he continued to seek peace because he knew it was out there somewhere and had hope of finding it.

The second dream took place on a Catholic campus with several nuns surrounding him. They sought shelter in a strongly built building. The nuns explained to him that the enemy was sent to destroy their sanctuary and would soon be flying overhead with fighter planes and weapons. The holy ground they occupied was soon penetrated with bullets and fire. David was relieved that they survived the attacks and that good prevailed over evil.

The next dream took place in a hospital room, which was in a high-rise building surrounded by water. He was located near the top floor. As David leaned out the window from his room, he saw small boats converged at the base of the square-shaped, straight-up, brick-sided building. The nurse explained the occupants in the boats wanted to convince David to go with them. She explained they were deceitful and spoke of lies.

Even though David realized they were evil, they were so convincing that it became harder to reject them. David knew he was located in a safe part of the building and the exterior building structure was slick, and he was assured they could not climb to his room. The nurse told him that these people would never give up trying to convince him to join them on their mission. The nurse encouraged David to be strong and reject them.

In another dream, David was on a hospital gurney talking to a nurse about how much he loved Hardee's biscuits. The nurse had a plan to get David to Hardee's early the next day before sunrise to be the first in line to get what he loved so much: a hot Hardee's breakfast biscuit. As he arrived, he could see a woman creating the delicious meal. David knew he was close to finally getting to enjoy a nice treat. As David was rolled into the building on his gurney, the woman told him that he could now receive his reward. As David was slowly rolled into position to receive his reward at the counter, he looked down and saw the wheels of the gurney going through several inches of tar. The closer he got to the counter, the deeper the tar.

The dream faded into another scene. David was in his hospital room and needed assistance from the nurse. He kept pressing the "nurse" button, but no nurse came. A nurse finally appeared, and he explained his need for her assistance. The nurse stated to David that she could not respond to his request unless he picked up the items on the floor. David leaned over the bed and saw sixes separated in groups of three. David knew he needed the nurse to help him, but was determined not to pick up the sixes. David explained he would rather die than pick up Satan's sixes. He knew he did not want to surrender to Satan.

David went into great detail on the next dream, which had little or no meaning, but was still so vivid in his mind. David was in a dark hallway with a low ceiling. The area was similar to a cave. As he stood for a lengthy time, he could hardly bear the low-pitched organ music.

All of a sudden, a woman appeared in a black gown and said, "Here she comes."

As the music got louder, a round-faced dwarf appeared, wearing a bright, yellow gown and headdress, shaped similar to an American Indian headdress. As she and her entourage marched by to the organ tunes, he asked the woman in the black gown who was the woman in the yellow gown. The response was shocking.

"You are attending Satan's wedding, and the woman in yellow is the devil's bride."

David stated he was frightened in the dream and woke up sweating. He was delighted the dream was over, but would never forget all the details of the horrible sights of evil.

I had a horrible experience that felt like a bad dream in David's room after the morphine was halted. David fought with all his might to make great strides in his physical therapy and daily routines like brushing his teeth and combing his hair. One morning, I assisted him in getting ready for his afternoon routine of dialysis and physical therapy, which took place in the bed. We were surprised to be greeted by a new nurse who was just assigned to the intensive care unit. She was a beautiful, young woman, but didn't appear to have confidence in taking care of David. She appeared nervous and rushed through the daily tasks of taking his vitals. Upon adjusting his many tubes and wires that encompassed him that day, she pulled the side rails to his bed in the upward position and pinched the breathing tube. Thank goodness I was there and on the opposite side of the bed from the nurse. David thrashed in the bed with his face turning blue—he had no oxygen. I immediately saw the pinched tube and screamed at the nurse to lower the bed rails. She panicked and left the room, and another nurse appeared. In the meantime, I grabbed the manual breathing apparatus from the head of the bed to apply to David's face so he could breathe while the nurse lowered the bed rails. What an adrenaline rush. After that incident, I felt like I lived through a nightmare that I will never forget.

I believe all the heartaches, trials, and drama in the intensive care unit was to strengthen our faith in God. I realized everything is in God's hands and I cannot control the outcome of anyone's health condition or life. I learned I needed to trust God to do His work for the good of all. For once in my life, I had to shut up, sit down, and let God do His job. As a person who is detail-oriented and likes to control and lead, I finally got it! I can't accomplish anything in life without God. That's right. It is all about God. The roller-coaster ride had just started, and I needed to learn from it and enjoy the journey.

"Trust in the Lord with all your heart and lean not on your own understanding; in all your ways acknowledge him, and he will make your paths straight." – Proverbs 3:5-6

6

Angel in the Parking Deck

———————— ⟨๑⟩ ————————

MCV hospital was my new home. David's liver transplant and recovery would take place in this massive educational hospital off Broad Street in downtown Richmond. Trying to find the correct hospital wing to report to and an open parking spot in the deck was frightening.

It's funny—with all the abnormalities in my life, the parking deck process was comforting only because I knew what to expect each day. When entering the massive deck, a machine issued a ticket. When leaving the deck at the end of the day, your ticket was validated by a receptionist inside the hospital for a cheaper rate.

Riding the elevator to the appropriate level to retrieve my car was an experience in itself. The elevator was always slow and packed with people from various cultures. All passengers in the elevator appeared to be tired, frustrated, sad, and lonely. I always smiled at the strangers, but I never received any acknowledgment—only silence.

I wonder why people stop talking when they are in the elevator; it always feels uncomfortable.

When finally reaching my vehicle, I would sit and try to focus on my next plan of action. I learned after David's diagnosis to take each moment as it came. I would usually gather my thoughts, money, and ticket for the deck-exiting process. At the exit ramp, there was a cashier in a small booth with only a tiny window to receive money and validated tickets. I never paid attention to the cashier because of my urgency to leave the hospital complex. Spending four to six hours after work or running back and forth to the hospital on my lunch break was so exhausting, and I missed my children.

There was only one cashier whom caught my attention. She was a small-framed woman with blonde hair. I called her my parking deck angel. She would always greet me with a smile, but never said much. She did mention to me that she only worked part-time there to earn money for her college education. She told me that she had two children at home and could only work part-time because of college. I admired and envied her for her drive and ability to see the future. At that point in my life, in my thirties and only married since 1984, I could not see a future for me, David, or my sons.

My angel always appeared to know what was happening with David, but I never told her his name or mine. David was on his deathbed several times during his many surgeries.

One particular day, the doctors told me that he would not live through the night. The next morning, when I arrived at the deck, my angel said, "David is alive!" She excitedly screamed, "We should name this facility the

Miracle Hospital of Virginia!" Immediately, I thought, *How could she possibly know David and his condition?*

After sitting in the waiting room that day waiting to speak to the doctors, I smiled, thinking of another miracle that happened in the hospital that same week. One night, I was on my knees beside my bed, praying God would hear my prayer and guide the hands of the surgeons and nursing staff or heal him. I frantically searched to hear God's voice. I sobbed so hard that I could not catch my breath. I needed God, I wanted to feel His presence, and I needed hope.

It was after midnight when the phone rang. It scared me, and I didn't want to answer. I tried to stop crying as I answered.

The caller said, "Pam, this is Audrey Gardner."

I was puzzled. *Why would David's supervisor's wife be calling me at this time of the night?*

She calmly said, "Focus on Jesus's face." Her calming voice and her sweet spirit soothed my soul. How did she know I had cried out to God? How did she know I needed comfort and wisdom? Was God using her to let me know He heard my prayer? Audrey quickly said she thought of me while she prayed for David and had to call.

Within a few minutes after I hung up the phone—I believe it was around 1:30 a.m.—the phone rang again. I was surprised to hear the hospital student chaplain on the line. Immediately, I thought David had died, but he quickly stated he was excited to share a miracle that took place in MCV with me. I took a deep breath, sighed from relief, and listened carefully. How did he know I needed hope?

At the start of the story, I felt goose bumps on the back of my neck, and tears of amazement trickled down my face. He began to tell the miracle with such excitement that he hardly took a breath between sentences. He quickly said there was a young boy of around seven years old who needed emergency surgery at MCV. The procedure was dangerous, and if the procedure failed, he would die. The boy needed a shunt inserted in his neck.

The chaplain was with the boy's mother, close to the surgical room, and could hear all the commotion. The surgeons were under a lot of stress to make sure this shunt was placed correctly. The surgeons talked among themselves, checked medical records, and were confused on where the shunt should be placed. The chaplain's voice cracked as if he cried as he told me that all of a sudden, a bright light was shown on the boy's neck as a sign where to place the shunt. The boy's eyes opened wide at the same time under deep anesthesia, and his face glowed. The surgery was a success, and the doctors approached the mother and chaplain with a big smile. The doctor said he was alive and well.

In the recovery room, the mother sobbed as she spoke to her son.

The boy said, "Mom, why are you crying? I am okay. I saw Jesus!"

The chaplain softly said, "Another miracle."

He apologized to me for calling so late, but he had to share this miracle from God. I thanked him and fell asleep with a big smile on my face. I had not smiled for months.

After another long day at the hospital, I headed for the parking deck, thinking I have an angel who waits for me. Her kindness and patience gave me hope and encouragement, especially on difficult days. Every day, when arriving to the hospital complex and especially the deck, I felt so isolated and in another world. Things did not feel real to me. I guess I ran on adrenaline and was bogged down with all my thoughts and emotions inside my heart.

Many times, I think I was angry at life in general. I released my anger one day in the parking deck after the doctors told me to go home. After being urged to leave at 1:00 a.m., I was scared to walk alone to the deck. Most people at this time of the morning would ask for an escort, but I didn't.

My car was located in the lowest level and parked in an extremely dark corner. I remember screaming to the top of my lungs, *"Make my day!"* I was so angry that I could have truly hurt someone. As I drove out of the deck, I couldn't remember how to get on I-95 to go home.

My car must have been guided by God to get me home safely. All I remember that night is I sang praise and worship songs all the way down I-95 without stopping. I remembered my father's wisdom even after all these years. He died of cancer when I was ten years old. He told me when I was scared, I should just sing, and I did. I sang words to songs I didn't know. The closer I got to my house, the louder I sang. I was always scared to see what waited for me at home—sad and crying children, leaky pipes, and unwanted bill collector messages demanding money I did not have. The bill collectors always threatened to take my house, my car, and everything I owned if I didn't pay my hospital bills. I always told them that the check was in the mail, and I would shout out loud after hanging up the phone, "You can't take my sense of humor." It was like Satan was on a mission to destroy my faith. I was determined to rebuke Satan and stand firm on the rock of Jesus Christ! I was in a battle every day at home, at the hospital, and at life in general. I was determined to win the fight.

After over six months in the hospital, David was finally released to come home. I searched frantically for my angel that day because I wanted David to meet her. I especially wanted to thank her for her kindness and support and celebrate David's homecoming. I could not find her in the whole deck. I rode through the deck several times. When I got home, I immediately called the hospital to ask for the supervisor of the parking attendants. Once the supervisor came to the phone, I asked him about the blonde, petite attendant who worked there to pay for her college education. I wanted to know her name and her schedule so I could send a thank-you gift/card. I told the supervisor about her encouraging smile and kindness. The supervisor laughed and told me that he did not have a blonde attendant and had not hired one in years. After the phone conversation ended, I started to think, *Maybe I have imagined her or maybe I am going crazy?* No! She was there for me as my sign of hope.

"Jesus looked at them and said, 'With man this is impossible, but not with God; all things are possible with God.'" –Mark 10:27

7

Waiting Room Friends

⸻⟨♥⟩⸻

The waiting room outside the trauma unit at MCV was always crowded. I spent many hours in this room just to be close to David. I never wanted to leave him because I didn't want to miss the opportunity to speak to him if he awoke from his induced coma.

One day, I came into the waiting room and saw a man whom I recognized. I said hello and introduced myself to him. It was David Reynolds. I worked for Reynolds Metals Company at the time and realized he was the CEO. We immediately started talking. I told him that my husband was in the trauma unit due to two liver transplants, and he shared his wife was there with heart issues.

I then told him that I worked for his company and was grateful for my great job and all the wonderful employees. I actually mentioned I had only missed a few days from work due to David's illness. I explained working was the best medicine for me. It didn't mean I didn't care for my husband; it meant I had a distraction from all the craziness. I felt halfway normal at work.

After that day, I had the pleasure of seeing Mr. Reynolds almost every day for a number of weeks. I felt so sorry for him. I realized during this time that no other family member joined him. He looked so tired and sad, and I wanted to do something special for him.

I decided that a brown-bag lunch might be a special treat for a wealthy man who was catered to at work. Mr. Reynolds had special staff who prepared his daily meals in an elegant dining room. I wanted him to know I was his friend and had empathy for him. I remember my father telling me that anyone who has a lot of money would never know whom his or her true friends were.

Late that night, I went home and placed a peanut butter and jelly sandwich, a bag of chips, and a snack cake in a brown paper bag. I put a napkin in the bag and sealed the bag with a special prayer.

I wanted Mr. Reynolds to know how special he was by giving him a down-to-earth, friendly lunch from an ordinary, plain lady. I didn't want anything from him, and I didn't want him to remember my name. I wanted him to feel loved. He smiled at me when I handed him the lunch bag. I smiled back at him while watching him enjoy the lunch and the act of kindness.

Several times, I would meet him in the hospital hallways, and he would spin me around and was so excited to tell me his wife was better. I was so happy for him, but jealous at the same time because David was still in the same coma. By his smile, I felt he appreciated our short-lived friendship.

Several weeks later, I saw Mr. Reynolds with his head in his hands, crying. I knew at that moment that his wife had passed away. He looked at me and was speechless. My heart ached for him because I knew he had hope several weeks ago. At that moment, I began to panic, thinking I would soon face the same news of death. I immediately stopped thinking that and started to pray. I asked God to continue to protect David from all diseases and infections. I asked him to continue to heal him so we could go home to our precious boys.

Several weeks later, my insurance nightmare began. I assumed Mr. Reynolds went back to his office and went on a personnel search for my name. He probably wondered if Reynolds Metals Company paid for my husband's $2.5-million costs for surgeries.

At this time in my life, I was exhausted with the insurance issue. If I had to give advice to anyone who has a terminal disease, I would recommend seeking an attorney as soon as you receive a diagnosis. There were times that I would go to get David's anti-rejection medicine at the pharmacy, which he could not live without, and the pharmacist would say the insurance company denied the prescription. I am a pretty understanding woman, but when it comes to a life-or-death situation regarding my family, I turn into a crazy woman. Once, I threw my body across the pharmacy counter and grabbed a pharmacist by his lab coat. I shouted from the top of my lungs to give me the medicine or I would have his job. That is out of character for me, but at times, I took drastic measures in order to fight for my husband and our boys. I had had enough with the insurance circus, and now I would take action.

I wrote a letter explaining my insurance frustration to the White House, and they called me personally to respond and told me to contact them if my issue was not resolved. I also copied Virginia Senators Chuck Robb and Mark Warner and Congressman Thomas Bliley, Jr. All recipients of my letter responded immediately and informed me that they contacted all insurance companies involved and the State Corporation Commission. I truly believe they got the ball rolling on resolving the issue.

I soon received a request to represent Reynolds Metals Company in a suit against Southern Health. *Cooper v. Southern Health* grievance hearing was on July 12, 1993. I was promised if I did so, I would never have to worry about losing my job at Reynolds Metals Company. That was not true because I lost my job in 1998. When I was escorted to my car, I saw about thirty other employees in the parking lot. I then realized all of us or our spouses had medical problems. My heart was broken because I was a faithful employee for nineteen and a half years. I did not have time to grieve; I needed to immediately seek a job to support my family.

From the grievance hearing in July 1993 until the end of 1995, I was in and out of court due to this crazy insurance nightmare. Bill collectors would call me in the middle of the night demanding checks. They harassed me, even on holidays. I got to the point that I would tell them that the $2.5-million check was in the mail.

After David's second transplant, the most heart-breaking experience was trying to get disability for him from Social Security. David was so weak and sick; he could hardly walk. We appeared together in front of a judge to plead for disability. The judge thought I was

David's lawyer because I had on a business suit and carried a briefcase. The judge asked me a few questions and realized I was his wife, not his attorney. The judge was curt and ordered us to obtain a lawyer. Before we left the courtroom, he humiliated David by asking medical questions in front of the room full of people. Questions pertaining to his bowel movements and personal lifestyle. David was so embarrassed, and I was angry. We left in a hurry, and we both broke down in tears when we entered our car to go home.

Now, with little money, I had to find an attorney to fight for him. We needed his disability income to live. David was seen by Social Security doctors and psychiatrists and went through a pile of medical forms. Through lawyers and paperwork, David was denied disability.

For a man who could not walk, talk, went blind for six months, and couldn't be left alone, disability was denied. To this day, I cannot believe it happened. They denied him because his sight came back enough that he could find a job answering the phone. Seriously? The man could not even hold up his underwear.

I kept encouraging David to fight. I went out and purchased a puppy to give him company, asked neighbors to check in on him, and changed my dining room into a bedroom so David could be on the first floor of our home and near the kitchen. I paid a handyman to upgrade our half bath to a handicap one so David would be more comfortable.

After receiving numerous letters from collection agencies, my settlement agreement was finally done in late 1995. The state waived a huge amount of the cost, and the rest of the bill was divided into thirds. MCV accepted the sum of $426,063.60 as payment in full, Southern Health agreed to pay MCV the sum of $212,281.81, and the Coopers would pay $1,500.00. The physician bills were compromised and also divided into thirds.

Finally, the stress was gone. I could concentrate on how to keep the house running on only my salary. I knew God was with us and He would provide.

"Do not be anxious about anything, but in every-thing, by prayer and petition, with thanksgiving, present your requests to God." – Philippians 4:6

8

Letter to the Donor's Family

It took me a while to write the donor's family a thank-you letter. I tried several times to write it, but could not find the words. I cried every time I picked up my pen. I so desperately wanted to personally meet the donor's family and thank them for their unconditional love.

I know this sounds crazy, but after David recuperated, he craved strawberries dipped in chocolate, insisted on baking at least two cakes a week, and enjoyed watching *The Martha Stewart Show*. I was shocked because he never ate chocolate-dipped strawberries or liked to bake. I laughed out loud every time he mentioned he was going to the kitchen to experiment with an exciting new recipe. David was not Martha Stewart, but he finally had an interest in something that kept him busy during the day while I worked.

I found it interesting that he received a female liver and took on female tendencies. We laughed together often about his lack of coordination when we danced. David would always say that maybe the donor would rather cook than dance. His great sense of humor kept our lives interesting.

Finally, on May 20, 1993, I typed my thank-you letter.

Dear Donor Family,

I have attempted to write this letter three times since June 22, 1992. I don't know where to begin to express my sincere appreciation for your love in giving an organ for my husband's life.

My husband, David, age thirty-nine, underwent two liver transplants back to back and had serious complications. Your loved one's organ combined with God's miracles spared his life. Your gift of life is a wonderful expression of brotherly love, and I will cherish your love and kindness forever.

A day doesn't go by that I don't think of your family and the pain you must carry in your heart. I have experienced this pain by losing my father at age ten. But knowing my father's body was used to help others lessened the pain.

As I watch David grow stronger each day, I thank God for your love and our many blessings. David, our two boys, and I will cherish your generosity forever.

God bless, Pam

I was relieved to have finally completed the letter. I would have preferred to meet the family and spend time, bonding while sharing family stories. I wanted our families to be close to share all the wonderful things that God had done in David's life. Protocol with transplant patients at MCV was to give the letter to the administrative staff at the hospital, and someone on staff would make sure the donor's family received the letter.

I was so disappointed that I never received a response from the donor's family. In my heart, I felt like I knew the donor by watching David's habits, interests, and personality change. She must have been an amazing lady with a great sense of humor and a taste for sweets.

"A gift opens the way for the giver and ushers him into the presence of the great." – Proverbs 18:16

9

Time to Live

After three years of recuperation, David began to live a normal life. First thing on his agenda was a job. Since his vision was still not good, opportunities were scarce. My sister Sandy and her husband Paul owned Ridout Homes Inc. and had an opening for a field supervisor to handle residential construction projects. They were so kind to offer him this position. This job gave David a chance to get back to the career he loved. His expertise was in commercial building, but residential construction was a start. He had plenty of experience as a union carpenter and was a building inspector with Chesterfield County prior to his illness. He was so excited to be able to provide for his family.

As David's strength increased, he had opportunities to advance in his career. He had the pleasure to work for DeFoggi Construction and build churches. Since God gave him a second chance at life, he felt like he wanted to give back to the community. He felt like building churches was a thank-you to God for all the miracles and blessings.

The happiest I have ever seen David was when he landed a job with our church, Clover Hill Assembly of God. He met Pastor Stan Grant while working for DeFoggi building the church. David looked at me during the groundbreaking ceremony at Clover Hill, and with tears in his eyes, he proclaimed we belonged at that church. In my heart, I felt the same. This would be our new church family.

Before I knew it, David was offered a position with Clover Hill as a facility manager who would be responsible for overseeing the addition of a new sanctuary. He accepted the offer, and it was an answer to my prayers. This is when I knew God was in control and had a great future for David.

The doctors told me after the second transplant that David would probably live a year, and it would be a miracle to live five years. God had other plans. He lived twenty-two years past the last diagnosis, and *that* is a miracle!

David was blessed to be able to work with the children at the Clover Hill Assembly of God Academy. He loved children of all ages. The children thought he was Superman. They called him Cooper. They watched him use his hands in repairing items in the church, clean bathrooms and floors, set up and break down chairs, and build projection screens and more using his mighty hammer. All the boys wanted Cooper to teach them how to hammer.

David was in heaven! He explained to me that working for God was his ticket. He always searched for something more and could never figure it out. Now, the mystery was solved. Serving God made him complete. His mission now was to make sure everyone he knew was saved. He wanted to ensure he saw everyone in heaven.

During these wonderful years of living life to the fullest, we watched Brian and Chris become successful in school and in sports. Both boys took up motorcycle racing, and several weekends a month, we took them to racetracks across Virginia. We started off camping in the car and finally had the money to purchase an RV. We pulled an enclosed trailer with two motorcycles, barrels of water, tools, and even our dog. We were called BC Racing Team.

Every chance we had, we made sure we hosted picnics or meals with the family, went to Virginia Beach, and enjoyed being a family. David still struggled with diabetes, kidney issues, and high blood pressure. Doctors thought he might need kidney dialysis or even a transplant. Upon that kidney diagnosis, I started to prepare David's man cave for the area to receive home dialysis, and I painted the closet in that room to make it sterile for the medication.

I could tell David struggled working long hours at the church, but it was his pleasure. I remember watching him stagger down the sidewalk at night and especially on Sunday evenings from exhaustion. He loved his job and gave it everything he had.

One evening, at our church small group meeting at our house, David received a call from a detective with Chesterfield County. After he hung up the phone, he looked at me with total shock, and his face was white as snow. He proceeded to tell me that he has been accused of sexually assaulting a little two-year-old boy at the church school. I could not believe what I heard. David didn't even know the boy because he had no dealings with that age group. How could this be happening? He would never hurt a soul, especially a child.

I sat in the truck and watched David go into the court-house to be questioned by the detective. My heart was breaking, and I cried out to God. I asked God to protect David and to give him strength, wisdom, and peace. David was a broken man. He came out of the detective's office with his head hanging, and tears flowed down his cheeks. This accusation started the downward spiral of his health.

I called the church to speak to the pastor. I could not believe someone accused David of something so horrible. It was so obvious with cameras and the presence of teachers that David was not guilty. The pastor encouraged "Coop" to be calm and tell the truth. What the pastor didn't understand is the accusation caused David's health to worsen. He could not sleep, eat, think, or stop crying. I found him in a fetal position, lying on the couch in the man cave. His bones started to show due to lack of nourishment. I felt he was dying. I immediately called my friends Renee and Scott from church and ask if they could come over to help me with David. Renee owns a health food store, and I knew she had some type of healthy remedy to help prevent his downward spiral. She and I made smoothies with vegetables, fruits, protein, and more. He finally started sipping on the drink, which gave us all hope.

Within a week, I started to see improvements. David began to build his strength so he could continue to work at the church. It was never the same after this horrible accusation. The children always greeted David every morning with a high-five and a big hug. He was afraid to touch or even hug a child. Every day was stressful for him until finally I demanded to meet the parents of this child. The meeting took place in the pastor's office. The mother, who was a school counselor, apologized to us for the accusation. Why did she accuse him in the first place? David and I stared at both parents in disbelief. Throughout the conversation, I held back the tears and anger. Finally, the pastor looked at David and told him it was up to him if the child should be removed from the academy. David calmly looked at the mother, who didn't attend our church, and informed her that the child needed to be at the loving academy, and he encouraged the parents to attend the church.

That moment was so special because it showed David's true character and his strength to forgive the parents. Soon after the meeting, David decided it was time to give up his job at the church. His health had worsened, and he had no energy. It was a sad day for both the church and us. Many hugs and well wishes were shared among the staff.

David continued to see various specialists regarding his condition and eventually ended up in the hospital for more testing. It was determined he needed to be removed from the hospital and sent home with hospice. I set up a hospital bed in the man cave and prepared daily to give him all the support, encouragement, and love that I had. I worked with the hospice staff and pharmacy to make sure he had the best quality of care. He was taken off all of his medications, and now all we had to do was manage the pain that he endured. Our son Brian lived out of town and that left our son Chris, David's sister Marlene, and David's father, Al, to help out so that I could continue to work.

Marlene quit her job at Kohl's to be able to spend time with David while I worked. His father visited often. Marlene and David became the best of friends as they watched TV together and shared snacks and his special orange-flavored drinks. It was great witnessing a brother and sister bonding and reminiscing their childhood days. During this time, we could not leave David alone. He became weaker by the day and started to get uncomfortable and disoriented.

Each time a hospice nurse arrived, I would pray they would give him a shot of something that would relieve his pain. He lost twenty pounds within weeks, and his bones started to protrude. He looked like he hadn't eaten in months. To this day, I truly believe he had liver cancer. He was cold all the time, even in the warmer weather. I would layer him in thermal underwear, several T-shirts, sweaters, coats, and neck scarves just to get him to church. He walked slowly with a cane, and his head began to droop. During this time, David started to lose his balance and fall.

As more and more pain medication arrived at the house, David became more agitated, uncomfortable, and anxious to get up. There were times that we had to restrain him in the bed. He was always looking at the ceiling smiling, frowning, and reaching for something in the air. I told him he saw angels and he tried to catch them. I would sit by his bed and read Scriptures, hold his hand, and kiss him on the forehead. I loved my husband more than life itself! It broke my heart to have to say good-bye, so I didn't. I painted a beautiful picture of heaven, as stated in the book of Revelation in the Bible, and told him we would be together soon for eternity.

Days and days went by, and the hospice nurses could not believe he was still alive. They couldn't figure out why he was still fighting. I truly believe he did not want to die at home because he knew I had to continue to live at the house.

Chris and I spent seven days with him without leaving the house. We would take shifts, giving him pain medications every thirty minutes, watching him struggle and not sleep as he continuously moved in the bed. We only ate if someone brought something to the house, and we slept in thirty-minute-or-less sessions. We were determined to never leave his side. My best friend Nancy, who is a nurse, came to the house after her shift to give us relief. She was so dedicated and never appeared tired as she comforted David. I think David calmed down and rested when he saw Nancy. Nancy and I had been friends since second grade, and David knew I loved her unconditionally, and he trusted her.

During the last week of David's life, I suffered from exhaustion, depression, dehydration, and bordered a nervous breakdown. I had back issues from lifting and turning David, and I was in severe pain and needed to see my chiropractor. I quickly made an appointment, but first needed to find someone to sit with David while I was in my treatment session. My sister Sandy and my sister-in-law Marlene agreed to assist.

Leaving the house was uncomfortable because I had not left David's side in weeks. I was frantic, thinking something would happen to him while I was gone. I stopped at a stoplight on Courthouse Road, and Satan then attacked. I felt a strong object on each shoulder that felt warm. This loud, sarcastic voice kept repeating, "Where is your God now? Where is your God now?"

I quickly realized it was Satan, and now the fight was on! I immediately started quoting Scripture and shouting to the top of my lungs that "Jesus is my Lord and Savior and I am standing on His word."

All of a sudden, I felt heavy objects leave my shoulders, and I heard a hissing sound. Tears of joy streamed down my face. It felt like the world stood still. I turned my head to my left and saw a man staring at me with eyes that were wide and bulging. The light changed, and I pressed the accelerator with zest. I started singing praise and worship songs out loud and thanked God for all His blessings.

As I pulled my car into the chiropractor's parking lot, pain shot down my lower back and legs. I slowly crawled out of my Honda Accord and wanted to collapse. I was weak from the stoplight event and in severe pain.

Dr. Kranski met me at the car, and I fell into his arms, crying. He encouraged me to walk with him to his office for a back treatment. After the treatment, he informed me that I was not to lift anymore. He stated my back was done. Dr. Kranski instructed me to walk around the parking lot slowly and that he would reevaluate me after the next patient. He and his staff were so accommodating and sweet to me as I left the office. It was clear I could not lift anymore.

I slowly walked to my car and was anxious to get home to David. I felt like I had been away from him for days. Upon arriving home, I found him in the floor surrounded by people. David had fallen out of his recliner, and it took several people to lift him back into his chair.

The next few days were his last. My friends Trina and Karen came to the house to fix food, encouraged me to sleep, and they spent time with David. I was scared to go to sleep, so Karen got in the bed with me to rub my back to relax me, and eventually, I dozed off. I felt like I was dying inside. I felt exhausted, but knew I had to keep fighting to keep David comfortable until the Lord took him home.

After seven days, Chris and I were both mentally and physically exhausted. We continued to be by his side as he became more restless. I stared across the bed rails to Chris and whispered it was time to call hospice and request them to transport his dad to Retreat Hospital in downtown Richmond. As the hospice transport team came into the house, I felt frightened. Deep inside, I knew it would be the last time David would leave our home. David looked so peaceful lying in his bright-orange T-shirt. That T-shirt was special to him. We had it designed in Virginia Beach.

On the back of the shirt was a cross with Jesus's face inside it. These T-shirts were worn as we competed with the boys on the racing circuit. It was a great way to spread the Gospel without speaking. I always told the boys that our actions on the racetrack spoke volumes over words. Brian and Chris wore the cross on the back of their racing helmets and always bowed their heads in prayer at the starting line. Before we knew it, the majority of the racers joined them.

David's sister Marlene and I immediately got in my car to travel to the hospital. When we walked into his room, he was up in the bed, cleaned and groomed. He didn't say anything, but he did give Marlene a huge smile, which brightened the room. David had a gap in his front teeth, which made his smile priceless. My heart was pounding as I neared him for a kiss. I kissed him gently on his forehead and smiled. I had all intentions to return early the next morning to spend every moment with him alone. That never happened.

At 3:00 the next morning, I received a call from the hospital. The nurse informed me that if I wanted to see David, I had to come immediately as his vital signs weakened. I knew it would take me an hour to get to the hospital from my house. I wanted to call a family member to ride with me, but realized I would not have enough time to pick them up and get to the hospital.

I crawled into the bed and began to pray out loud to God. I asked Him to take David home in loving fashion. I asked Him to wrap His loving arms around David for a big hug from me and the boys. At around 4:00 a.m., I received a call from Retreat that David passed peacefully. Even though I knew he would pass, my heart broke, and I cried uncontrollably. After calling the family and my pastor, I began to get dressed to go to the crematory to identify his body. Our son Chris and I rode together in silence to the crematory in downtown Richmond.

Upon seeing his body, we both wept in each other's arms. Chris and I had a hard time leaving David's body. We both wanted to hug him, but we were only allowed to view him through a glass window. Chris confirmed several times that his dad was finally at peace.

We both left the building with broken hearts, but relieved David was finally healed and in perfect form in heaven. We drove to P. F. Chang's at Stoney Point Shopping Center in Richmond for lunch and a cold beer. While the waiter took our order, Chris began to cry. The waiter didn't look uncomfortable and pressed in to ask if everything was okay. I explained we just lost David. The waiter was so emotional that he left our table. Chris and I snuggled close and talked quietly until our lunch arrived. At the end of the meal, the manager came over and told us that the waiter paid for our lunch. We were so touched.

Now it was time to prepare for David's memorial service at Clover Hill Assembly of God, which was two weeks after his death date. It was time to celebrate the life of this wonderful man, husband, and father.

> "So do not fear, for I am with you; do not be dismayed, for I am your God. I will strengthen you and help you; I will uphold you with my righteous right hand." – Isaiah 41:10

10

Unbroken

———————— ⌘ ————————

David's supervisor at Clover Hill Assembly of God, Sharon Wells, immediately took charge of organizing David's memorial service. She had given him a book titled *Unbroken* one year before his death. She told David that the book was about him. Sharon and David loved each other and shared survival stories. Sharon is a cancer survivor, and David prayed for her for years. Sharon was David's encourager and cheerleader. She based his memorial service on his unbroken testimony.

For David to be unbroken was to be ceaseless; undisturbed; solid and continuous. That is the way David Cooper lived his life. He was ceaseless in the tasks that needed to get done and the plans that needed to be fulfilled. He would work until his body would not allow him to any longer. He worked unbroken.

David was not disturbed by the trials and tests that came his way; he marched on, being a living testimony of God's grace, mercy, and healing power. He lived unbroken.

He was solid and continuous in his love of his Savior and the mission at hand. Even in the end, his concern was his family and friends would come to know the Savior he knew. His faith was unbroken.

He was a builder of many things, but his greatest achievement and the one he would want to be remembered for was what he could do to build the Kingdom. His body failed him, but his God never did. He left this world unbroken.

David's last wish was to make sure his memorial service was full of praise and worship, a message of salvation, and to celebrate his heavenly life. David's wish was fulfilled. The church sanctuary was full of family, friends, and even people we did not know. Ten people gave their life to Christ, and the church rocked with glorious praise and worship.

David left a legacy of unbroken love for his Lord and Savior.

"Do not let your hearts be troubled. Trust in God; trust also in me. In my Father's house are many rooms; if it were not so, I would have told you. I am going there to prepare a place for you."
–John 14:1-2